Random Fascinating Facts About Everything:

Interesting Facts About Pop Culture, Science, History and Everything Else

By Frank Baker

Introduction

Welcome to this book Random Fascinating Facts About Anything: Interesting Facts about Pop Culture, Science, History and Everything Else. Here you will read about a selection of specially chosen facts about a wide variety of topics - and hopefully learn something new about the world!

The Facts

The phrase 'worthy of your salt' comes from Roman times. Roman soldiers were paid part of their wages in salt because salt was used to preserve food.

-

The planets in the Solar System revolve around the centre of the mass of the solar system, which is very close to the Sun.

-

The apple pie was invented in England. The first recipe for apple pie dates back to 1381.

-

Thomas Edison just came up with a better version of the light bulb. The light bulb had already been invented.

-

The most common theories for the extinction of the dinosaurs are a catastrophic meteorite collision or an epidemic.

-

Artist Vincent Van Gogh cut off part of his ear lobe

in an argument with artist Paul Gauguin.

-

Even though it ended in 2004, the sitcom Friends is still the most streamed television show in the world.

-

It has been said that people eat around 10 spiders a year. This is due to things such as eating spiders during sleep, and spider in processed food.

-

The average person has three to five dreams a night. However, most of these dreams are completely forgotten or only half-remembered.

-

Walt Disney he was cremated upon his death in 1966 - not cryogenically frozen.

-

There are estimated to be 352 quintillion gallons of water in the Earth's oceans.

-

The food most people are allergic to is cow's milk.

-

There are believed to be millions of species of insects we haven't discovered yet.

-

Caffeine drinks such as coffee do not cause dehydration.

-

The Nazis developed jet fighters before the end of World War 2 but there were too few of these planes and insufficient fuel and pilots to make much difference to the outcome of the conflict.

-

It is said that one should not eat during a fever. But this has shown not be true and the immune system is helped by eating.

-

Royal Marines with night vision rifle scopes were deployed in the British national park Exmoor in 1983 after there were reported sightings of a puma.

-

The Muslim Jihad does not necessarily mean Holy

War in terms of war, but can mean a spiritual struggle unrelated to war.

-

The ring doughnut was invented in 1847. It was discovered by 15 year old Hanson Gregory cut the centre out of a fried doughnut.

-

A soldier captured by the Americans during the invasion of Normandy was initially thought to be Japanese but he was actually a Korean named Yang Kyoungjong who in 1938 had been forced to fight for the Japanese Kwantung Army in Manchuria. He was then captured by the Red Army during the battle of Khalkhin Gol in 1939 and forced to fight for the Soviet Union after spending time in a labour camp. In 1943, Kyoungjong was captured by the Germans during the Battle of Kharkov in the Ukraine and ended up in the Atlantic Wall near 'Utah Beach' as a German conscript where his incredible war finally came to an end with D-Day!

-

Humans started to live on earth 63 million years after the dinosaurs died out.

-

The sandwich is said to have been invented by

John Montagu, 4th Earl of Sandwich (who died in 1792). Legend has it that Lord Sandwich was always too busy to eat a proper meal so had his servants bring him slices of meat and bread while he worked. He then put the bread and meat together - thus inventing the sandwich!

-

-

Nazi is a colloquial word in German that means foolish, which is why critics of the Nazis called them this.

-

Superman made his debut in Action Comics #1 in 1938. Superman creators Jerry Siegel and Joe Shuster never made much money from their iconic creation and were felt to be harshly treated (especially by film studios) when it came to sharing profits. Jimmy Olsen and Kryptonite were actually creations of the radio series rather than the comic.

-

It is said that Wolfgang Amadeus Mozart composed Twinkle Twinkle Little Star when he was five years old. But the tune is from an old French folk song, and Mozart composed a tune based on it.

-

Butterbeer in Harry Potter is a drink made with butterscotch. It is probably based on a real beverage called Buttered Beer which was drunk in Tudor times. Buttered beer was made with beer, eggs, sugar, nutmegs and cloves.

-

The closest US state to Africa is in Maine - on a peninsula called Quoddy Head.

-

There are around 40,000 known spider species.

-

Peanuts are from a plant and not really nuts. They are a legume.

-

The legendary singer Elvis Presley became notorious for his food binges near the end of his life. His favourite snack was a preposterously huge sandwich that contained bacon, peanut butter and strawberry jam.

It is estimated that one of these sandwiches contained 42,000 calories and Elvis was known to eat two of them a day!

-

In popular culture ninjas always wear black. In reality they wore clothing that allows them to blend into specific situations.

-

India was the source of diamonds until the early 18th century. Diamonds fields were then discovered in Brazil and then - in 1867 - in South Africa.

-

Although humans share 99% of DNA with apes they were not descended from them. They shared a common ancestor from which apes and humans descended.

-

Astronomers believe there are about 100 thousand million stars in the Milky Way alone.

-

Only 8% of body heat is lost through the head during cold weather.

-

Mary Shelley was only eighteen years-old when she began writing Frankenstein.

-

McDonald's first chicken item was the McChicken sandwich. It was introduced in 1980. The new chicken dish was not very popular at first.

-

-

Cheap brown bread is similar to white bread, and includes food colouring and some extra added fibre.

-

Tom Selleck was the first actor cast as Indiana Jones for the 1981 film Raiders of the Lost Ark. Selleck then became unavailable because of a scheduling clash with his new TV show Magnum so Harrison Ford became Indiana Jones instead.

-

Humans have 20 senses such as hunger and temperature.

-

In 2020, it was reported that a newly discovered species of snake in India was given the name Salazar Slytherin in tribute to Harry Potter.

-

Many people believe that slaves built the pyramids. But in fact the job was considered an honour so paid professional labourers were employed.

-

The nations in the world who possess nuclear weapons are the United States, Russia, China, Great Britain, France, India, and Pakistan. North Korea and Israel are believed to have nuclear weapons but their capabilities remain vague and secretive.

-

Diamonds come from compressed carbon which is deeper under the earth than coal.

-

Mike Tyson is the youngest boxer to win a version of the world heavyweight championship. Tyson was twenty years-old when he beat Trevor Berbick to win the WBC title in 1986.

-

The McDonald's Happy Meal was first introduced to restaurants in 1979.

-

The Great Wall of China can not actually be seen from space with the naked eye.

-

The Argentinosaurus huinculensis is believed to have been the largest dinosaur. It is estimated to have have been as heavy as 90 metric tons.

-

French Queen Antoinette is quoted as saying about starving peasants "let them eat cake" - or brioche, a sweet bread. But this quote was made up in a satirical piece by Jean-Jacques Rousseau.

-

The books which have sold more than a hundred million copies are A Tale of Two Cities, The Hobbit, Harry Potter and the Philosopher's Stone, And Then There Were None, The Little Prince, and Dream of the Red Chamber.

-

Bats actually have good eyesight. They have small eyes and can see three times better than humans.

-

A hybristophiliac is a person who is strangely attracted to people alleged to have committed extreme crimes. This condition would explain the weird phenomenon of serial killers developing pen pals while in prison.

-

Jesus was not born on December 25th. The Bible says it may have been in September. Pope Julius the First chose the 25h December in 350AD to coincide with various existing winter festivals.

-

Some conspiracy theorists still maintain that NASA hoaxed the moon landings. They believe that 1960s technology was too primitive to stage a moon landing and that the whole thing was staged in a television studio.

-

Giving children too much sugar does not cause hyperactivity.

-

The Catcher in the Rye is one of the most banned books in American history.

-

People with blue eyes take longer to get drunk.

-

Sarah Woodson was the first African American woman to graduate from college. She studied at Oberlin College and graduated in 1856.

-

Meteorites are a cold when they enter the Earth atmosphere. Heat removes the outside layer and when they land on Earth they are cool.

-

The Greek philosopher Thales predicted the eclipse of May 585 BC.

-

Bats actually have good eyesight. They have small eyes and can see three times better than humans.

-

There are 49 landlocked countries in the world. This means they have no coast, beaches, or access to the sea.

-

-

Yogurt is said to be good for digestion because of the bacteria in it. But because bacteria in the digestive system is not understood, the benefits of yogurt are unproven.

-

The engineer Gustave Eiffel designed the Eiffel Tower as the focal point of the Paris exhibition of 1889. The tower elicited protests when it was finished from locals who thought it was an eyesore.

\-

Humans are born with 300 bones, but this decreases to 206 at adulthood.

\-

Apples were introduced to North America by people who emigrated there from Europe.

\-

Charles Schulz, who created Charlie Brown and snoopy, disliked the newspapers calling his comic strip 'Peanuts'. The Charlie Brown comics started in the fifties as 'Li'l Folks' but the newspaper syndicate changed the name. Peanuts was eventually read by 300 million readers in 75 countries.

\-

Jupiter, Neptune and Uranus all have rings around them.

\-

The first familiar name in English literature was Chaucer. Chaucer is credited with the re-establishment of English as a native language.

\-

Water makes up about 80% of the human body.

-

Ian Fleming, the creator of the James Bond novels, complained when Sean Connery was cast as his literary hero in the first James Bond film. He said Connery looked like a truck driver. Fleming changed his mind when he saw the film and gave Bond some Scottish ancestry in tribute to Connery.

-

When Uranus was discovered in 1781 it was actually called Georgium Sidus - George's Star. It was then named after the Greek God Uranus in 1850.

-

The most common explanations for UFO sightings are satellites, shooting stars, natural atmospheric phenomena, aircraft, and the planet Venus.

-

Bananas grow on a banana plant - not a tree.

-

The Taj Mahal is a tomb built by the Mogul Emperor of India to house the body of his late wife. The Taj is made of white marble.

-

The 100 Years War actually lasted for 116 years.

-

Frank Wathernam was the last prisoner to leave Alcatraz prison. He was released on the 21st of March 1963.

-

The people in the USA take over half of the aspirin tablets in the World.

-

It is thought that red makes bulls angry. But in fact bulls are colour blind. Waving and movements make them angry.

-

The Battle of Britain began on July the 10th 1940. Nazi Germany could only invade Great Britain by sea and land if they first had control of the skies. This task fell to the Luftwaffe (the German air force) but they never managed to achieve this thanks to the dogged resistance put up by the pilots of the Royal Air Force. Hitler abandoned plans to invade Britain and decided to concentrate on the invasion of the Soviet Union. The bravery of the British and Allied pilots in the Battle of

Britain led to one of Winston Churchill's most famous quotes - 'Never in the field of human conflict have so many owed so much to so few.'

-

The most eaten food in the world is rice.

-

Golf was played over various numbers of holes per round until St. Andrews course in Scotland settled on an 18 hole course in 1764.

-

On Halloween night in Britain in 1992, the BBC broadcast a show called Ghostwatch. It was a one-off scripted drama about an investigation into an alleged haunted house. Ghostwatch used real television presenters and was designed to look like a genuine 'live broadcast' investigation show. Many viewers seemed unaware that Ghostwatch had been a fictional drama though and the BBC were deluged with complaints from the public for broadcasting something so terrifying. Ghostwatch was so controversial that it was never broadcast on British television again.

-

Bananas grow towards the sun. This causes them grow into a curved shape.

Dell Computers was founded by a 19 year who had $1000 in capital.

-

When it was first released, the book Harry Potter and the Deathly Hallows sold 8 million copies in 24 hours.

-

In popular culture ninjas always wear black. In reality they wore clothing that allows them to blend into specific situations.

-

Dreams are essentially hallucinations which occur during different cycles of sleep.

-

NASA - the US space agency - gets about 1% of the Government's budget every year.

-

As of 2020, the footballer Cristiano Ronaldo is the most followed person on Instagram. He has nearly 230 million followers.

-

Adam and Eve famously ate a forbidden apple from the tree of knowledge in the Bible. But it just says it is a forbidden fruit and not specifically an an apple.

-

Jack the Ripper was a serial killer who operated in the Whitechapel district of London in 1888. He killed five women in gruesome fashion. The reason why this killer is so enduringly famous is that he (or she?) was never caught. To this day we do not know who Jack the Ripper really was. This has led to endless speculation and theories over the true identity of the Ripper. Some believe it was a Masonic or Royal conspiracy and new Ripper suspects continue to abound to this day.

-

-

Famous Egyptian ruler Cleopatra was actually Macedonian-Greek.

-

Whiskers on cats are there so that the cat can judge spaces and see if a gap is big enough to pass through. It is a myth that cats need whiskers to maintain a sense of balance.

-

The full name of the US city of Los Angles is "El Pueblo de Nuestra Senora la Reina de los Angeles de Porciuncula."

-

Expressionist art is a movement where painters express their inner feelings rather than depict the world as it appears to the eye. The two big inspirations for expressionist art are Van Gogh and Edvard Munch.

-

Death by spider bites are very rare in Australia.

-

The first cooking television show in America was broadcast on the 30th August 1946. The show was called I Love to Eat - it ran for 15 minutes and was hosted by James Beard.

-

The longest running sitcom in the world was a

BBC show called Last of the Summer Wine. It ran from 1973 to 2010.

-

D-Day was the name given to the Allied invasion of Nazi controlled continental Europe in World War 2. It was launched on June the 6th 1944 from England. The invasion was called Operation Overlord and targeted an 80km area of the Normandy coast in France. D-day is the largest invasion by sea in history.

-

If the sun was made of coal it would burn to ashes in 5000 years.

-

Salty Water has a higher boiling point than normal drinking water.

-

Early telescopes were refractors. Isaac Newton presented the first reflector telescope in 1671.

-

Fish have a five month memory.

-

Atlantis was first mentioned in Plato's dialogues Timaeus and Critias. It is alleged to have been an advanced civilisation that perished and now resides under the sea somewhere.

Many have searched for Atlantis but no conclusive evidence for its existence was ever found.

-

Juiced fruit and veg removes some of the natural fibre.

-

The Vatican is the Palace of Popes. Since 1929 the Vatican has been an independent sovereign country within Italy.

-

It is illegal to sell a haunted house in New York without informing the buyer it is haunted.

-

Barbarossa was the codename for the invasion of the Soviet Union by Nazi Germany on the 22nd of June 1941. Barbarossa or Red Beard was a term for Emperor Frederick I. Three million German soldiers were involved in the initial invasion and although it began with great success, the material and manpower resources of the Soviet Union were eventually too vast for the Germans to overcome.

The decision to invade the Soviet Union is regarded by most historians to be the biggest mistake Hitler made during the war.

-

The first restaurant opened by McDonald's founder Patrick McDonald was The Airdrome. It was a food stand on Route 66 in the US and opened in 1937.

-

28 year-old Ruth Ellis was the last woman to be sentenced to death in Britain. She was hung in 1955 for murdering her boyfriend. The punishment received much criticism and hastened the abolition of capital punishment in Britain. By 1964 the death penalty had been abolished.

-

Bulgarians nod when they mean no, and shake their head when they mean yes.

-

The serial killer Rodney Alcala became known as The Dating Game killer because in 1978, before he was captured, he appeared on the television game show The Dating Game as one of the bachelors hoping to win a date with the female contestant. Luckily for the woman in question, she didn't pick Alcala to be her date!

-

The first animals in space were fruit flies. They were sent into space in a V-2 rocket by the USA in 1947. The flies survived the flight.

-

A French woman named Jeanne Calment was the oldest recorded person. She lived to be 122 years-old. She was born in 1875 and died three years before the 21st century started!

-

-

Brown sugar contains molasses which have some extra minerals and vitamins. But it is really the same as white sugar and it not healthier.

-

Christopher Columbus was responsible for introducing the lemon to America in 1493.

-

The HG Wells book The War of the Worlds, where Martians invade England, was inspired by the way Imperial Powers treated less advanced nations and the way mankind wreaks destruction on the animal kingdom.

-

Women have twice the pain receptors as men, but also have more tolerance of pain than men.

-

Coconuts kill 160 people each year.

-

The cartoon character on the Pringle's snack tubes is called Julius.

-

The deadliest ant in the world is the bulldog ant (Myrmecia pyriformis) found in Australia.

-

Lasagne originated in Medieval England.

-

A person who reads in bed is called a A librocubicularist.

-

Pisces, Virgo, Sagittarius and Gemini and the most common signs of serial killers. They are all mutable signs.

-

A heart beats three billion times in the average human lifespan.

-

Shaving legs does not make hair grow back quicker.

-

KFC started using the short form of their name instead of Kentucky Fried Chicken in 1991. They believed Fried might put people off the brand.

-

OJ Simpson was the studio choice to play the T-100 cyborg that made Arnold Schwarzenegger famous in The Terminator.

-

In Saratoga Springs in New York in 1853, a cook

called George Crum served very thin slices of fried potato after a customer complained that the potatoes were sliced too thickly. Potato chips were first called Saratoga Chips as a result. Then from the early 20th century potato crisps were mass produced in factories.

-

It is said that tryptophan - an amino acid in turkey - makes people relax after eating it. But a lot of the acid has to be consumed before it induces drowsiness. Also the acid is present in other common foods such as cheese.

-

The McDonalds Big Mac was first introduced in 1968.

-

The most expensive hamburger in the World is the Honkytonk burger from Galmburger in London. It costs about $1500 and contains expensive kobe and wagyu beef, lobster, caviar, gold leaf, truffle, a duck egg and venison.

-

Some of the Inca Sun Temples have stones fitted so perfectly you couldn't place a knife between them.

-

A bullet fired straight up in the air will lose velocity on the way down so will not be lethal if it hits someone.

-

More salt is used to de-ice roads than season food.

-

Most scientists and astronomers believe it is statistically plausible that aliens exist but do not believe they have ever visited Earth.

-

KFC was the first western fast food franchise to open a restaurant in in China. A restaurant opened in 1987.

-

Bagpipes actually originate from the middle east.

-

Reykjavik, the Icelandic capital, is warmer than Chicago in the winter.

-

A Virginia park ranger named Roy C. Sullivan was struck by lightning seven different times. Ironically, after surviving seven lightning strikes, he committed suicide in 1983 because of an unhappy love life.

-

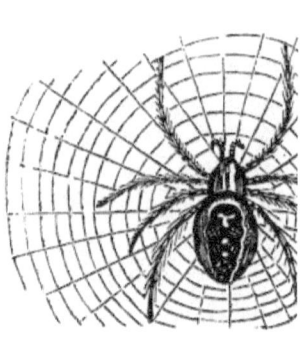

-

The word coconut comes from a name which was given to it by Portuguese sailors when they discovered it in the 1500s. The name is "coco", which means grinning face.

-

St Paul's Cathedral was built by Christopher Wren between 1675 and 1710 on Ludgate hill to replace a cathedral destroyed in the Great Fire of London.

-

Balls in the NFL for one season require leather from 3000 cows.

-

The Japanese military practised cannibalism near the end of World War 2. The Allied authorities knew of this but suppressed the details when the war ended for fear of upsetting relatives of lost soldiers.

-

SOS, the distress signal, does not mean save our ship. SOS was chosen as it is an easy morse code signal - three dots, three dashes, three dots.

-

The legendary sprinter Jesse Owens was so broke after he retired from athletics that he worked in a gas station at one point.

-

Humans do use all of their brain but not all at the same time. Certain areas of the brain are used for specific tasks as one time.

-

The Tintin books by Hergé have sold over 200 million copies in 70 different languages.

-

Coca Cola has never been green, but it was once sold in green bottles.

-

Phillis Wheatley was the first African American to publish a book of poems.

-

Hippopotamus milk is coloured pink.

-

Aerosmith have made more from Guitar Hero - the game - than they have made from album sales.

-

The Hound of the Baskervilles was inspired by Arthur Conan Doyle's fascination with Dartmoor (a rugged area of natural beauty in England). Conan Doyle took many walks through Dartmoor and heard of the legends and myths associated with this land. Although he had killed off Sherlock Holmes, he felt the idea of a Holmes mystery set on Dartmoor was too good not to write.

-

Mice do not like cheese, and prefer fruit, vegetables and grains.

\-

When he wrote his novel Carrie, Stephen King was broke and working in a laundry. He threw the manuscript in the trash but his wife fished it out and it became a bestseller.

\-

The modern Internet was introduced in 1990 with the World Wide Web. It was invented by Tim Berners Lee. It introduced HTTP, a web browser, HTML - a coding language, and web server.

\-

There is no evidence that Vitamin C helps fight a cold.

\-

The largest kidney stone ever recorded weighed 2.9 pounds (1.36kg).

\-

Bruce Willis only got the part of John McClane in Die Hard because Richard Gere, Mel Gibson and Sly Stallone turned it down.

\-

The first USB flash drives were introduced in 2000.

-

The name Jessica was invented by Shakespeare. It first appeared in The Merchant of Venice.

-

In the classic black and white Hitchcock chiller Psycho, chocolate sauce was used to depict blood when Janet Leigh is stabbed in the shower.

-

The first ever KFC chicken restaurant was opened in a petrol station in North Corbin, Kentucky in 1930.

-

Landscaped tidy gardens are not good for the environment. A wild overgrown garden is much greener because it creates an ecosystem for birds and insects.

-

Dogs can understand 250 gestures and words.

-

The Golden Arches, The McDonalds logo, was designed by architect Stanley Clark Meston in 1952.

-

The legendary Hollywood film star Cary Grant was British in real life. He was born in Bristol, England.

-

Tomatoes are a fruit and not a vegetable.

-

-

The Maginot Line was a series of fortifications built by the French in the 1930s to protect themselves from any German aggression. It was manned by the French army and even had its own subway system. It proved to be completely useless in World War 2 though because the Germans aimed the focal point of their attack at the Ardennes region of Belgium and simply bypassed the Maginot Line.

-

Workers spend about 45 hours per year defecating during work hours.

-

Cabbage is 91% water.

-

Galileo Galilei made scientific observations concerning the moon and stars from 1610. He constructed his own telescope which had a magnification of x30.

-

Alcohol makes the veins pump warm blood to the skin at the expense of core body heat, so in fact heat is lost.

-

None of the names of the USA states contain the letter Q.

-

The sun's energy derives from nuclear transformations at its core.

-

Pluto is is not completely dark as he Sun's rays still reach it.

-

More than 200 supposed cases of spontaneous human combustion have been reported.

-

Meat free diets provide enough nutrition, including protein.

-

Although the 1979 film Manhattan is one of his most acclaimed pictures, Woody Allen hated the movie so much he tried to buy the rights off United Artists so that no one would be able to watch it.

-

S is the letter which has the most words in starting with it in the English language.

-

The cast of Friends were paid an astonishing one million dollars per episode for the tenth and final season.

-

At the Salem Witch Trials of 1692 suspected witches were hanged or crushed to death.

-

The shells of Armadillos are bullet proof.

-

A day was only 21 hours long 620 million years ago.

-

In 1992, Mae Jemison became the first African American woman in space when the space shuttle Endeavour ferried her and six other astronauts on orbits around the Earth.

-

The Sun is actually white. When looked at low in the sky on Earth it looks orange and other shades because of atmospheric scattering - radiation from the Sun in the atmosphere.

-

The first black athlete ever to appear in the Olympics was the Frenchman Constantin Henriquez de Zubiera in 1900.

-

Human bodies glow in the dark. Human eyes are too weak to see this.

-

Archaeology digs have unearthed Chinese metals that pre-date western science by 1,500 years.

-

The iconic Welcome to Fabulous Las Vegas sign was erected in 1959.

-

Nine out of ten people struck by lightning survive because direct strikes are very rare.

-

Raindrops fall at 7 mph/11 kph.

-

Jingle Bells, the famous Christmas song, was originally a song written for the November American Thanksgiving festival.

-

70% of the red meat eaten in the world is goat meat.

-

About 60000 people are on an aeroplane in the

US at any one time.

-

Carrots have Vitamin A which helps eyesight.
They can only improve eyesight if a person has
Vitamin A deficiency.

-

The first air display took place in Paris in 1783.
The display consisted of one passenger in a hot air
balloon.

-

You can prevent crying when chopping an onion
chew gum.

-

There are now over 8000 different varieties of
apple grown in the world.

-

Batman was invented by Bob Kane and Bill Finger
and made his first appearance in Detective Comics
#27 in May 1939. Kane was inspired by Leonardo
da Vinci drawings which depicted a flying machine
with gigantic bat wings.

-

A human being produces enough spit to fill two swimming pools during their lifetime.

-

The average person eats about 2lbs (1kg) of insects every year - they are accidentally ground up in jams and sauces.

-

-

Some historians argue that the Second World War really began in 1931 with the Japanese invasion of Manchuria.

-

Pasta was introduced to Italy by Arabs in the 7th Century.

-

Blood accounts for 8% of the body weight of a

human being.

-

Printer ink costs more than Dom Perignon champagne.

-

The human brain is capable of 38 thousand trillion operations per second; the most powerful supercomputer can only manage .003 percent of the human brain.

-

In 1933 Kiyoko Matsumoto jumped to his death into a volcano on the Japanese island of Oshima. Others started to copy him, and 300 children did the same thing.

-

Cats are known as the gymnasts of the animal world for good reason. They can even pivot in mid-air to ensure a safe landing.

-

The first laptops were introduced in 1981. They were the Osborne 1 and Epsom HX-20. They had a 5 inch screen.

-

Half a million animals are killed for meat every hour in the USA.

-

The Mary Celeste is the name of a cargo ship that sailed from New York in 1872. It was discovered seaworthy off Gibraltar a month later. The only problem was that the crew had completely vanished. One of the most common theories is that a hallucinogenic fungus in the ship's supply of rye bread drove the crew mad and made them jump overboard.

-

Frankenstein is not the name of the monster. It's creator was called Frankenstein.

-

Although the most American of authors, Raymond Chandler was raised in England. His iconic detective Philip Marlowe was named after Marlowe House in Dulwich College where Chandler went to school.

-

French Emperor Napoleon was five feet six, which was an average height for a Frenchman in the late 18th Century.

-

A person can live up to a week without water.

-

There are 7 octillion atoms in the human body.

-

Ice-skater Debi Thomas was the first African American to win a medal at the Winter Olympics. She took a bronze in the 1988 Winter Games.

-

The capital city of Australia is Canberra in the Australian Capital Territory State.

-

There is a theory that spontaneous human combustion may be created by ball lightning.

-

Sushi does not mean raw fish, but in fact sushi means "sour tasting" in Japanese.

-

Stonehenge is astronomically aligned.

-

Butterflies use their feet to taste food.

-

People with tattoos are estimated to be around six times more likely to have hepatitis C.

-

Worms do not become two worms when cut in half. Only the front half can survive.

-

At one point during the First World War, Adolf Hitler and Winston Churchill were only a few trenches away from each other.

-

Earth is the only planet in the Solar System not named after a God.

-

3D movies were first invented in 1915.

-

In the early 20th Century, the Guzman prize offered a reward for anyone who made contact with aliens. Mars was excluded from the competition because it was deemed too easy to contact Martians - such was the confidence that life existed on Mars.

-

A wet nose has nothing to do with a dog's health.

-

The internet or 'world wide web' was invented by a British computer scientist named Tim Berners-Lee in 1989.

-

Mount Everest is called the tallest mountain in the world because you can stand at its base and summit. But Mauna Kea on Hawaii is higher - much of It Is underwater.

-

-

The atoms that were formed during the Big Bang

are the atoms present in human bodies.

-

Cats have 32 muscles in their ears.

-

The first meal eaten by a human on the moon was canned peaches.

-

The Nazca Lines fall across the Nazca plains of Peru. It is speculated that they represent a celestial calendar but some believe it was a runway for alien spaceships.

-

Chewing gum passes through the body in the normal way with non indigestible parts exiting the body in the usual way.

-

90% of the World's species that have become extinct have been types of bird.

-

The original Buddha from Buddhist culture was not fat. The big Buddha image comes from Budai who was a 10th century Chinese folk hero.

-

The Lake Champlain Monster is a sea creature (rather like the Loch Ness Monster) alleged to reside in a fresh water lake on the American/Canadian border. PT Barnum once offered a reward for anyone who could capture the monster.

-

There is no evidence to suggest that Vikings wore horned helmets. They were depicted wearing them in later art and operas.

-

Coca-Cola famously became New Coke in 1985 and were deluged with complaints from angry Americans. There is a conspiracy theory that it was all a ruse to allow the company to put cheaper ingredients in Coca-Cola when it (inevitably) made its return.

-

Processed cheese slices only contain 50% of cheese.

-

In 1917 two young girls in England produced photographs of themselves with some fairies in their garden. A lot of people who probably should have known better (including Arthur Conan Doyle) got very excited by the notion that fairies had been captured in a photograph but it was, of course, revealed many years later as a hoax.

-

The Hague is called the capital of the Netherlands because it has the Parliament, supreme Court and other Dutch government agencies. But constitutionally Amsterdam is called the Dutch capital.

-

The Elgin Theatre in Ottawa in Canada introduced a second screen in 1957. By doing so it became the World's first multi screen cinema.

-

Youtube was launched in 2005.

-

The heavyweight boxer Tommy Morrison, who starred in Rocky V, had to retire in 1996 when he tested positive for AIDS during a medical. Leaked medical files later suggested that he might have had AIDS since 1989.

-

Microwave ovens do not give off enough energy to damage human cells and cause cancer.

-

Oranges are green in some areas of the world.

-

WhatsApp was sold to Facebook for 19 billion dollars. A few years before the sale Facebook turned down the WhatsApp creators application for a job.

-

The human brain is capable of reading 100 words a minute.

-

In 1845, Captain Sir John Franklin's launched an expedition to search for the North West Passage from the Atlantic to the Pacific, something that had eluded explorers for two centuries. No one knows what happened to the two ships that made up the expedition but all these years later men from the expedition are still sometimes found buried and preserved in the ice. The preserved body of Petty Officer John Torrington was found after it been buried in the Arctic ice for 140 years.

-

French philosopher Voltaire did not actually write this famous phrase: "I disapprove of what you say, but I will defend to the death your right to say it."

It was written by English writer Evelyn Beatrice Hall.

-

A scene in the sitcom Friends where Chandler Bing makes a joke about a bomb at an airport had to be deleted when the 9/11 attack occurred.

-

The conspiracy theorist David Icke suggested that the Royal Family were shape shifting lizards who drank human blood.

-

The traditional cowboy hat did not become popular in the American west until the end of the 1800s. Bowler or derby hats were more popular.

-

The first version of Windows was Windows 1.0. It was introduced in 1985.

-

Aristotle was the first person to supply evidence

that the Earth is a globe.

-

The radon and polonium in the smoke us what causes cancer from smoking.

-

President Rosevelt was confined to a wheelchair but most Americans were unaware of this because the wheelchair was always hidden when he appeared in newsreel footage.

-

Buckingham Palace has 775 rooms, 19 state rooms, 52 royal and guest bedrooms, 188 staff bedrooms, 92 offices and 78 bathrooms.

-

Did aliens crash land in the desert near Roswell, New Mexico, in July 1947? Conspiracy theorists claim extraterrestrial beings and wreckage from their craft were found and taken but the military maintained it was debris from an experimental high-altitude surveillance balloon belonging to a classified project.

-

The ancient Egyptian alphabet contained 700 hieroglyphs.

-

Many television laugh tracks used in contemporary television shows were actually recorded in the 1950s.

-

Coffee is really made from the seed of the coffee plant.

-

Buckingham Palace was bought by the Royal family in 1761. George III paid £21000. This is about £3 million in today's money. Queen Victoria moved in in 1927 and named it as an official royal residence.

-

The Arctic explorer Matthew Henson was the navigator on a 1909 expedition to Greenland which might have been the first to reach the Geographic North Pole. Although a veteran of several expeditions, Henson was written out of history because he was black.

-

There are around 40 million olive tress on the Greek island of Crete.

A black belt is not necessarily the highest award in martial arts. Some disciplines have higher black belt ranks and higher belts such as red and white striped ones.

-

White witches in England lent their psychic powers to the Battle of Britain. The witches threw a substance known as 'go-away' powder into the sea.

-

-

Children of twins are genetically half siblings.

-

Most of the toilet paper sold in France is coloured pink.

-

Sean Connery decided to quit James Bond when a Japanese fan followed him into the toilet to ask for an autograph during the production of You Only Live Twice.

-

People should drink when they are thirsty, and drinking lots of extra water does not have extra health benefits.

-

Martin Bormann apparently sent a flight of stocks, patents, gold, bonds and copyrights out of Germany when he deduced the war was lost. The money moved through Switzerland alone would be worth trillions of dollars today.

-

10 percent of humans are left handed.

-

The mask worn by Michael Myers in the classic 1978 film Halloween was a Captain Kirk Star Trek toy mask that the production team purchased in a store and spray painted.

-

Around 1% of the World's population are drunk at the same time.

-

The word nerd was invented by the author Dr. Seuss.

-

As a businessman in the 1980s, Donald Trump would lure boxing matches to his Atlantic City casino. He was instrumental in putting together the big Tyson v Spinks fight in 1988.

-

Waking a sleepwalker will not cause any harm.

-

The human brain remembers more negative memories than positive ones as a defence mechanism.

-

It has been calculated that 28,000 of 40,000 U-boat sailors were killed in the Battle of Atlantic.

-

Fortune cookies were actually invented in the US in the early 1900s, and the fortune cookie tradition is actually Japanese; Japanese immigrants brought it to the US.

-

A number of swastikas formed by trees have been found in numerous forests in Germany. The swastika patterns could only be observed from above in certain seasons. Their origins remain a mystery but a logical theory is that the seeds were planted in a swastika pattern in the 1930s to celebrate Hitler's birthday.

-

Frozen food is frozen once it is picked, so it is better than store bought fresh food storing the nutrients until they are eaten.

-

Ian Fleming thought that stirring drinks damaged the flavour - which inspired James Bond's familiar shaken not stirred mantra when ordering his iconic vodka martini.

-

Leonard Digges built a working telescope in England in 1550.

-

Car maker Henry Ford is credited with inventing

the assembly line. This is not true as the assembly line has been used for thousands of years.

-

Baseball was inspired by Rounders - a near identical game that has been played in England since Tudor times.

-

The first President of the US George Washington lost his teeth in his 20s. He had dentures made of various items as gold, horse teeth and ivory.

-

The great novelist F. Scott Fitzgerald was an alcoholic and later humiliatingly had to eke out a living as a scriptwriter in Hollywood. He dropped dead at the age of 44 while eating a candy bar.

19,890 French civilians were killed during the liberation of Normandy.

-

Vikings have long been depicted drinking alcohol from their victims skull. But they did not actually do this - the idea came from a mistranslation of a Viking poem.

-

Google - the web browser - was created in 1998.

-

The film type that burns the most calories when watching is horror. Heart rate and adrenaline is increased.

-

The board game Dungeons & Dragons created a moral panic for supposedly glorifying witchcraft and the occult.

-

The IRS has a handbook about how to collect taxes after a nuclear war.

-

If you search for "do a barrel roll" on Google search the page spins round.

-

Muhammad Ali is one of the most beloved sporting icons of all time but as a young man he was unpopular because he converted to the Nation of Islam (a black separatist group) and then refused the draft ordering him to fight in Vietnam. Ali was banned from boxing for three years at the age of 27. In the 1970s, when he fought again, Ali became a much loved icon and because the Vietnam war proved so unpopular and disastrous, most people now felt that he had been right to protest against the draft.

-

The McDonald's advertising phrase "I'm loving it" was devised by Justin Timberlake.

-

-

The manager of Elvis Presley was "Colonel" Tom Parker - or Andreas Cornelis van Kuijk to give his real name. Parker was actually a Dutchman who moved to the United States as a young man and went to great lengths to hide his true identity and masquerade as an American. This is often cited as the reason why he would never allow Elvis to perform shows abroad, lest his true origin be revealed.

-

A billion seconds is 31 years.

-

The Aztecs in Mexico ate the bodies of their victims in human sacrifice rituals.

-

Roman chariot racing driver Gailus Appeuleius Diocles received the equivalent of 15 billion dollars in prize money during his career.

-

Percy Lavon Julian was the first African American chemist to be inducted into the National Academy of Sciences. Julian was an expert in the chemical synthesis of medicinal drugs from plants.

-

A dot leaf is an ancient remedy for a nettle sting.

-

50% of people in the World have never used a telephone.

-

The comedian Richard Pryor grew up in a brothel because his mother was a prostitute.

-

As a landlocked country, Switzerland doesn't have a navy but it does maintain a a flotilla of military patrol boats to police the lakes in Switzerland.

-

The first baseball club started in 1845.

-

Cheese does create more vivid dreams, but not predominantly nightmares.

-

Anthony Daniels and Kenny Baker, who played C-3PO and R2D2 in the Star Wars films, hated each other in real life. Kenny Baker said that Daniels was rude and condescending to him.

-

The orbiting section of the Viking 1 probe revealed what appeared to be a huge human face on the surface of Mars. It was most likely just a natural feature of the surface rock.

-

The table fork was invented in England in 1601. Before its invention people instead used a spoon or their fingers.

-

The Battle of the Bulge is also known as the Ardennes Offensive. This was the last major German offensive of World War 2. The aim of the offensive was to capture the port of Antwerp in Belgium and split the American and British forces. Hitler believed that the Allies would lose their appetite for war as a consequence and it would then allow him to transfer men and tanks to the east where they were badly needed to fight the Soviet Union. But with the Germans lacking experienced battle hardened soldiers and desperately short of fuel for tanks and vehicles, the offensive quickly petered out and fell hopelessly short of expectations. All it did was shorten the war because German armies in the west were now even weaker after the losses in men and tanks.

-

During World War 2, three million people were trapped in the siege of Leningrad. The German army surrounded the Soviet city with a blockade designed to starve the inhabitants to death. People got so hungry they even ate wallpaper. By the end of the siege, 260 Leningraders were arrested for cannibalism.

-

Sean Connery turned down the part of Gandalf in Peter Jackson's Lord of the Rings because he didn't understand the script. He had been offered 15% of the profits of the film so missed out on many millions by declining the role.

-

Einstein failed an entrance exam at the Zurich Federal Polytechnic School aged 16 because of his weakness in non mathematical subjects.

-

The great horror actor Vincent Price liked to go out trick or treating at Halloween.

-

The first country to leave what is now called the European Union was Greenland. Greenland left in 1982 after a referendum because the people didn't want the European Commission to control the fishing rights in Greenland's waters.

-

Canned herring is called sardines as the process was invented in Sardinia in Italy.

-

The phrase "No rest for the wicked" is often quoted from the Bible. But this saying is not in the

Bible. The line from Isaiah 57:21 is: "There is no peace, saith my God, to the wicked."

-

Sherlock Holmes was inspired by Sgt Cuff in the Wilkie Collins novel The Moonstone.

-

Oil does nor stop pasta from sticking when it is boiling in the pan, but it does prevent the water from boiling over.

-

Alligators can live for up to 100 years.

-

Joeseph Goebbels, Hitler's infamous propaganda minister, had a club foot.

-

Human fingernails look like they grow after death. But this is because the skin shrinks making it look like the fingernails are bigger.

-

London is the only city which has hosted the summer Olympic Games on three occasions: in 1908, 1948 and 2012.

-

The dwarves in The Wizard of Oz were said to be very badly behaved offscreen.

-

The first McDonald's in Scotland opened in 1987.

-

-

During their invasion of the Soviet Union, the German soldiers would sometimes find themselves fighting in snow over a metre deep in a temperature of minus 30 degrees.

-

It is said that having sex in the run up to participating in a sports event degrades performance. But it does not - as long as it is not just before the event.

-

The shortest war in history was the Anglo-Zanzibar War on the 27th August 1896. It lasted 39 minutes. It was fought between the United Kingdom and the Zanzibar Sultanate.

-

When someone is in pain and swears, the swearing releases endorphins that kill pain.

-

At Easter 1930 BBC radio in Britain said on a news broadcast "there is no news" and simply played a selection of music instead.

-

Ice Cream makers Ben and Jerry learnt to make ice cream via a correspondence course. It cost $5 to do the course.

-

Water makes up 96% of a cucumber.

-

The World's most grown plant is wheat.

-

Joseph Priestly invented carbonated water in 1767.

He also discovered oxygen.

-

Willian Semple invented chewing gum in 1896.

-

Coca-cola was named after a Corsican coco wine and the African kola nut, which provided the caffeine in Coca-cola.

-

The toothbrush was invented in China in 1498. The toothbrush bristles were made out of pig hair.

-

Theophilus Van Kannel invented The revolving door in Philadelphia in 1888.

-

There is no desert in Europe, making it the only continent in the World without a desert.

-

Fried chicken is the most popular meal eaten in

restaurants in the US.

-

No word in the English language rhymes with purple.

-

Confectionery maker M&M was named after the founders of the company Mars & Murrie.

-

The habit where people pick their nose too much is called Rhinotillexomania.

-

Potato chips - or crisps - with different flavourings were invented in the 1950's. Joe Murphy, the owner of Irish company Tayto, developed a technology to add seasoning to the crisps during manufacture in a factory.

-

Children who had a persistent cough used to be treated by heroin.

-

In World War 2, sliced bread was banned in the US.

-

Tabasco Sauce does not cause cancer.

-

Mayonnaise was invented by the Duke de Richelieu in 1756.

He wanted to make a sauce of cream and eggs mixed together as part of a celebration meal celebrating the French victory over the British at Port Mahon. He had no cream so used olive oil instead - and called it Mahonnaise.

-

The Earths surface is two thirds covered by water.

-

James Bond actor Daniel loves the British instant noodle snack Pot Noodle. During the filming of Bond movies he will often eat several each day.

-

Iceland is made up of lava from volcanoes. A thirds of the lave created in the world since 1500 has been in Iceland.

-

Ball lightening is an atmospheric electrical phenomenon.

The lightening balls are of different sizes - from the size of a pea to 11 metres in diameter. The balls can move through glass without breaking the glass.

-

In Western Europe. one third of coffee drank is made from coffee pods.

-

Victoria Woodhull was the first woman candidate for US President. She stood in 1876.

-

If a human drinks 100 cups of coffee over the space of four hours it will be fatal.

-

George Jung invented the fortune cookie in 1916. He was a noodle maker working in Los Angeles, USA.

-

The World's most expensive spice is saffron. Saffron is made from the dried stamens of the crocus flower.

-

The 1927 film The Jazz Singer was the first film with sound.

-

People were suspicious of potatoes when they were introduced to Europe in the 1600s. Yhey were thought to be poisonous.

-

One third of the World's coffee is produced in Brazil.

-

Cocoa - used to make chocolate - is mostly produced in Western Africa. Western Africa produces two thirds of the cocoa used in the World.

-

The potato chip or crisp was made popular by a cookbook called The Cook's Oracle by William Kitchine which was published in 1917.

-

The first two flavours of potato chips to be commercially produced were salt and vinegar and cheese and onion.

-

A bolt of lightening is almost four times hotter than the sun.

-

-

A four leaf clover is considered to be good luck for those who have one.

-

The average human being gets through 56 sheets of toilet paper every day.

-

Mushrooms are made up of 90% water.

-

Apples originated from central Asia.

-

The word potato comes from Spanish word –
patata.

-

Corn is added to soda drinks such as coco-cola as
a sweetener.

-

Christopher Columbus never visited the
continental north America on his voyages between
1492 and 1503, just various Caribbean islands
and Mexico.

-

If you placed all the strawberries grown every
year in a line, they would go round the Earth 17
times.

-

15000 people living in the Czech Republic said
their religion is Jedi.

-

An average cloud weighs around a million pounds
(450000 kg).

-

The human body has about 60000 miles (96000 km) of blood vessels - which if placed in a line could go round the world twice.

-

The famous detective fiction writer Agatha Christie stated that she came up with most of her plots whilst having a bath.

-

There are about 16 million ants to every human.

-

The story about the Three wise men visiting the baby Jesus and giving three gifts is well known. But the bible makes no mention of how many wise men visited, but as three gifts were given it is assumed there were three wise men.

-

Tsumtomu Yamaguchi was present in both Hiroshima and Nagasaki when the atomic bombs were dropped on the cities in Japan. He managed to survive both of the blasts and lived to the age of 93.

-

The founders of Google attempted to sell the company for around a million dollars in 1999.

-

The city of Portland in Oregon was chosen by the toss of a coin. The other choice for the name was Boston.

-

Russia has a bigger total land area than the planet of Pluto.

-

The tug of war used to be in the Olympic Games as an event.

-

The original name of the technology company Google was Blackrub.

-

A quarter of the population of the US have appeared on television at some point.

-

A person laughs about on average about 5 times a day.

-

A sneeze comes out of a person's mouth at the speed of about 600mph (965kmh).

-

The word for the alcoholic beverage brandy comes from the Dutch word brandewijn. It means burnt wine.

-

Dynamite has peanuts as one of its ingredients.

-

The Cambodian language has the largest alphabet; it consists of 74 letters.

-

The Catholic Church is the largest owner of land in New York City.

-

If a man never shaved the beard would be about 28ft (8.5 metres).

-

Bananas are attracted to people who have recently eaten mosquitoes.

-

When tomato ketchup was first sold in the 1880s it was sold as a medicine.

-

The fear of the number 13 is called Triskaidekaphobia.

-

A snail can hibernate for long periods - they can sleep for three years.

-

On average men speak 2000 words a day. Women speak 7000.

-

Cats have more than 100 different vocal sounds.

-

All the names of the continents on Earth start and end with the same letter.

-

The only month that does not have a full moon is February.

-

The anti-depressant lithium used to an ingredients of the soda drink 7-Up.

-

On average a McDonald's burger bun has 179 sesame seeds on it.

-

If all the numbers on a roulette wheel are added together, the total comes to 666.

-

Humans are outnumbered by insects on Earth by 1000000000 to 1.

-

Robert Zimmerman is the real name of the singer Bob Dylan.

-

Neil Armstrong, the first man on the Moon, first stepped on the Moon with his left foot.

-

8lbs (3.5kg) is the average weight of a human

head.

-

A human blinks on average about 6 million times a year.

-

There are about 100000 hairs on the average human scalp.

-

-

A Lemon contains more sugar than a strawberry.

-

Humans have on average about 1500 dreams per year.

-

If pearls are placed in vinegar they will melt.

-

McDonald's fast food restaurant use one third of all the beef produced in the US.

-

The largest hailstone ever recorded was about the size of a basketball.

-

50 bibles are sold every minute in the World.

-

The full name of the Thailand capital city of Bangkok is Krung Thep Mahanakhon Amon Rattanakosin Mahinthara Ayuthaya Mahadilok Phop Noppharat Ratchathani Burirom Udomratchaniwet Mahasathan Amon Piman Awatan Sathit Sakkathattiya Witsanukam Prasit.

-

Venice has 417 bridges in total.

-

KFC founder Harlan Sanders was not an actual colonel in the army, but a colonel of the state of Kentucky.

—

The first television cooking show was broadcast on the 12th June 1946 in Britain on the BBC. Cook Philip Harben presented a 10 minute show called Cookery. He cooked lobster vol au vents.

—

The first game show broadcast was The Pop Question Game. It was broadcast on American radio in 1923.

—

Herbert Hoover became the first US politician to appear on television. He appeared in 1927 in a demonstration of television. His voice and image was broadcast via telephone wires.

—

The first televised baseball game in the US was shown in 1939.

—

The first US television talk show was the Tonight Show on NBC. It was first broadcast in 1952.

—

Sortie de l'usine Lumière de Lyon, directed by

Louis and Auguste Lumière and released in 1894, is considered to be the first ever movie.

-

Half of the world's population eat rice with every meal.

-

The first cinema was the Berlin Wintergarden theatre in Berlin in Germany. The Skladanowsky brothers showed a short film at the theatre in 1895.

-

The first US television talk show was the Tonight Show on NBC. It was first broadcast in 1952.

-

Robert De Niro's favourite soup is asparagus.

-

The first CD available for sale in the US was Bruce Springsteen's Born in the USA.

-

A pencil contains enough lead for 50000 words.

-

Scotland has the biggest number of people with red hair.

-

Latvia is the country with the highest female population - 54%.

-

McDonald's Egg McMuffin was first served in 1972.

-

The alphabet of the Hawaiian language has only 12 letters.

-

Adults laugh on average about 17 times a day. Children laugh about 300 times per day.

-

It takes 1792 steps to climb to the top of the Eiffel Tower in Paris.

-

A quarter of the human body's bones are located in the feet.

-

There are no mosquitoes living in Iceland.

-

Vacuum, continuum and residuum are the only three words in the English language with a double u.

-

Light travels from the sun to the Earth in about eight minutes.

-

People type 56% of the time using their left hand.

-

Cats are not mentioned once in the Bible.

-

One fifth of the World's population earns a salary of less than $200 per year.

-

There are 293 different ways to receive change for a dollar.

-

The fruit banana comes from the same plant family as orchids, lilies and palms.

-

Laughing burns off about 4 calories.

-

-

The yo-yo toy was invented by Donald F. Duncan in 1929. He based his design a weapon used by Filipino hunters.

-

Mohammed is the most common name in the world.

-

The River Nile is the longest river in the World. It is 4145 miles (6670 km) long.

-

Angel Falls in Venezuela is the biggest waterfall in the world. It has a drop of 3121 feet (951 metres).

-

The first interracial kiss on television was between Kirk and Uhuru on the science fiction series Star Trek.

-

The last person to be killed by guillotine in France was Hamida Djandoubi.

He was executed in 1977. France abolished the death penalty in 1981.

-

Bigfoot is a huge seven foot tall upright ape creature said to mostly reside in the forests of the American Pacific Northwest. The most famous Bigfoot footage was shot by Roger Patterson in 1967. Most people think Bigfoot is simply a myth but alleged sightings still abound.

-

Wolves became extinct in Britain in 1743.

-

Elvis Presley's last ever concert was staged in Indianapolis in June 1977. The last song he ever sang was Bridge Over Troubled Water.

-

The last ever Peanuts cartoon strip was published on February 13, 2000.

-

Cricket used to be an Olympic sport. It last appeared in the Olympics at the Paris games in 1900.

-

Cigarette advertising was banned on radio and television in the US in 1971.

-

The last trial for witchcraft in England was in 1712. Jane Wenham was tried and found not guilty.

-

Jim Jones and the 900 followers in his Peoples Temple cult in Guyana in South America committed suicide by drinking kool aid mixed with cyanide.

-

Every continent has a McDonald's restaurant except for Antarctica.

-

At the ancient Olympic Games in Greece competitors competed in the nude.

-

At the 1912 Olympic Games in Stockholm, Sweden in 1912 the gold medals were actually made of solid gold. This was the last Olympics to do this.

-

Cherophobia is the fear of having fun.

-

The black truffle is more expensive than the white truffle.

-

Movie trailers used to be shown after the movie had finished. This is why they are called trailers.

-

If a human being broke wind for 7 years in a row the energy created would be the same as an atomic bomb.

-

An arctophile is a collector of teddy bears.

-

The last person to be executed in the Tower of London was the German spy Josef Jakobs. He was executed in 1941.

-

At the first modern Olympics held in Athens in 1886, the silver medals were awarded to the winners.

-

A human walks about twice around the world in an average lifetime.

-

The bible is the world's most shop lifted book.

-

The world's most expensive chocolate is from Knipschildt, a Danish manufacturer. They have a chocolate that costs $300 which contains black truffle.

-

In Japan Ronald McDonald - the McDonald's restaurant's mascot - is called Donald McDonald. It is easier to pronounce.

-

The world's largest clam ever recorded weighed 500lb (225kg).

-

On Mars the sunsets are blue.

-

True Lies made in 1994 was the first movie ever to have a budget of over $100 million.

-

In the early part of the 20th century lobster was a food only eaten by poor people.

-

Tea bags were invented in 1908 by Thomas Sullivan. He sent different teas to customers in small silk bags. People thought the bag had to be placed in water to make the tea - and the tea bag was born.

-

The bat is the only mammal that can fly.

-

Alligators, crocodiles, whales, dolphins, and turtles are creatures that live in the water and must come to the surface or they will drown.

-

Humans spend about 40 days of their life brushing their teeth.

-

The first McDonalds restaurant in Europe opened in 1971 in the Netherlands.

-

Truffles are one of the most expensive foods in the world. The fungi costs around $1.50 per lb (500kg).

-

The floppy disc for PC computers was first released in 1978.

-

The granny smith apple was invented in Australia in 1868 by Maria Ann Smith.

-

Buckingham Palace has 760 light bulbs. They are cleaned every six months.

-

-

The Apple Ipad was launched in 2010.

-

Honey never goes off.

-

On Saturn and Jupiter it rains diamonds.

-

In the bible Satan kills 2 people. God kills 10 million.

-

Gravity free rooms can cause flatulence.

-

The first ever video game was Tennis for Two. It was written in 1958.

-

Human eyes remain the same size after birth.

-

McDonalds sells 75 hamburgers per second, 6.5 million a day and 2.5 billion a year.

-

The average amount gambled by visitors to Las Vegas is $500.

-

A person in the US eats on average 35 tons of food in their lifetime.

-

Subway is the fast food company which has the most worldwide outlets.

-

The "Breakfast is the Most Important Meal of the Day" saying was invented by a cereal company in 1944.

-

Jupiter has 67 moons.

-

The first liquid propellant rocket was fired in 1926 by an American engineer named Robert Hutchings.

-

Bananas share 50% of DNA with humans.

-

When the caffeine is taken out of coffee to make decaffeinated coffee, the caffeine is sold to pharmaceutical companies

-

The human body contains 0.2mg of gold in the blood.

-

The ancient Egyptians invented toothpaste.

-

Women are six times less likely to be struck by lightening that men.

-

Tim Burton famously tried to make a Superman movie in the 1990s which would have starred Nicholas Cage as Superman. $50 million was spent on developing the film but it never went before the cameras because Warner Bros decided to cancel the project. You could have made two or three films with that money!

-

Coca Cola is a green colour before the black colouring is added.

-

Humans breathe about 8,409,600 times per year.

-

Ostrich eyes are bigger than ostrich brains.

-

If a person had 1 cent and doubled it every day, after 27 days that person would be a millionaire.

-

A person can live up to a month without food.

-

When fruit is dried about 60% of the vitamin and antioxidant content is lost.

-

Every day 50% of Americans are on a diet.

-

If you search for "askew" on Google search the results page will be slightly tilted to the right.

-

Licking a stamp gives 0.1 of a calorie.

-

50% of adults in the US eat a sandwich every day.

-

Birds do not urinate.

-

In 1926 a restaurant owner in Los Angeles was looking for a way to use up leftover celery, avocado, chives, tomato, watercress, chicken, bacon and Roquefort cheese. He placed them in a bowl and named the dish the Cobb salad.

-

A glass ball can bounce higher than a rubber ball.

-

-

The last time a wooden tennis racquet was used at the Wimbledon tennis championships was in 1987.

-

Villagers in China use dinosaur bones as a medicine.

-

Walt Disney is the second largest buyer of explosives in the world after the US military.

-

A Violin contains 70 bits of separate wood.

-

The first person to become a billionaire from writing books was J.K. Rowling, the author of the Harry Potter series.

-

When Coca-cola was invented, it only sold 25 bottles in its first year.

-

In today's money, a first class ticket on the Titanic would cost $100000.

-

A million seconds is 11 days.

-

Leonardo Da Vinci was a vegetarian.

-

The human eye can see 10million colours.

-

Saudi Arabia imports camels and sand.

\-

80% of creatures on Earth have six legs.

\-

The last official bare knuckle boxing match took place in 1889. John L. Sullivan beat Jake Kilrain by knocking him out in the 75th round

\-

A protein rich diet can cause problems in the liver and kidneys, and a balanced diet is better.

\-

Ted Bundy, one of the most evil and prolific serial killers in American history, once worked as the Assistant Director of the Seattle Crime Prevention Advisory Commission.